*GREATER ~~~~~~~~
ALSO AVAILABLE IN EBOOK AND
AUDIOBOOK FORMAT.

Greater Than a Tourist Book Series Reviews from Readers

I think the series is wonderful and beneficial for tourists to get information before visiting the city.

-Seckin Zumbul, Izmir Turkey

I am a world traveler who has read many trip guides but this one really made a difference for me. I would call it a heartfelt creation of a local guide expert instead of just a guide.

-Susy, Isla Holbox, Mexico

New to the area like me, this is a must have!

 -Joe, Bloomington, USA

This is a good series that gets down to it when looking for things to do at your destination without having to read a novel for just a few ideas.

-Rachel, Monterey, USA

Good information to have to plan my trip to this destination.

-Pennie Farrell, Mexico

Great ideas for a port day.

-Mary Martin USA

Aptly titled, you won't just be a tourist after reading this book. You'll be greater than a tourist!

-Alan Warner, Grand Rapids, USA

Even though I only have three days to spend in San Miguel in an upcoming visit, I will use the author's suggestions to guide some of my time there. An easy read - with chapters named to guide me in directions I want to go.

-Robert Catapano, USA

Great insights from a local perspective! Useful information and a very good value!

-Sarah, USA

This series provides an in-depth experience through the eyes of a local. Reading these series will help you to travel the city in with confidence and it'll make your journey a unique one.

-Andrew Teoh, Ipoh, Malaysia

>TOURIST

GREATER THAN A TOURIST- MISSOULA MONTANA USA

50 Travel Tips from a Local

Ella Rehder

Greater Than a Tourist- Missoula Montana USA Copyright © 2021 by CZYK Publishing LLC. All Rights Reserved.

All rights reserved. No part of this book may be reproduced in any form or by any electronic or mechanical means including information storage and retrieval systems, without permission in writing from the author. The only exception is by a reviewer, who may quote short excerpts in a review.
The statements in this book are of the authors and may not be the views of CZYK Publishing or Greater Than a Tourist.
First Edition
Cover designed by: Ivana Stamenkovic
Cover Image: provided by author
Image 1: By Edward Blake -
https://www.flickr.com/photos/eblake/8160155983/, CC BY 2.0,
https://commons.wikimedia.org/w/index.php?curid=31304532
Image 2: By PD photo.org -
http://pdphoto.org/PictureDetail.php?mat=&pg=7753, CC0,
https://commons.wikimedia.org/w/index.php?curid=12378762
Image 3: By prizrak2084 -
https://www.flickr.com/photos/prizrak2084/185172706/sizes/z/in/photostream/, CC BY 2.0, https://commons.wikimedia.org/w/index.php?curid=23823980
Image 4: By Alaskaair - Own work, CC BY-SA 3.0,
https://commons.wikimedia.org/w/index.php?curid=31401509

CZYK
PUBLISHING

CZYK Publishing Since 2011.
CZYKPublishing.com
Greater Than a Tourist

Lock Haven, PA
All rights reserved.
ISBN: 9798749202489

>TOURIST

50 TRAVEL TIPS FROM A LOCAL

BOOK DESCRIPTION

With travel tips and culture in our guidebooks written by a local, it is never too late to visit Missoula. Greater Than a Tourist- Missoula, Montana USA by Author Ella Rehder offers the inside scoop on Missoula, Montana, and all its uniqueness. Most travel books tell you how to travel like a tourist. Although there is nothing wrong with that, as part of the 'Greater Than a Tourist' series, this book will give you candid travel tips from someone who has lived at your next travel destination. This guide book will not tell you exact addresses or store hours but instead gives you knowledge that you may not find in other smaller print travel books. Experience cultural, culinary delights, and attractions with the guidance of a Local. Slow down and get to know the people with this invaluable guide. By the time you finish this book, you will be eager and prepared to discover new activities at your next travel destination.

Inside this travel guide book you will find:

Visitor information from a Local
Tour ideas and inspiration
Save time with valuable guidebook information

Greater Than a Tourist- A Travel Guidebook with 50 Travel Tips from a Local. Slow down, stay in one place, and get to know the people and culture. By the time you finish this book, you will be eager and prepared to travel to your next destination.

\>TOURIST

OUR STORY

Traveling is a passion of the Greater than a Tourist book series creator. Lisa studied abroad in college, and for their honeymoon Lisa and her husband toured Europe. During her travels to Malta, an older man tried to give her some advice based on his own experience living on the island since he was a young boy. She was not sure if she should talk to the stranger but was interested in his advice. When traveling to some places she was wary to talk to locals because she was afraid that they weren't being genuine. Through her travels, Lisa learned how much locals had to share with tourists. Lisa created the Greater Than a Tourist book series to help connect people with locals. A topic that locals are very passionate about sharing.

>TOURIST

TABLE OF CONTENTS

Book Description

Our Story

Table of Contents

Dedication

About the Author

How to Use This Book

From the Publisher

WELCOME TO > TOURIST

1. Watch The River Surfers at Caras Park
2. Take A Walk Down to Big Dipper Ice Cream For A Refreshing Treat
3. Ride 'A Carousel For Missoula'
4. Take A Walk In The Historic Downtown District
5. Visit The Saturday Farmer's Market
6. Eat Breakfast At The Catalyst Café
7. Go Hiking In The Rattlesnake National Recreation Area & Wilderness
8. Watch The Montana Sunset
9. Visit The Art Museum Or An Art Gallery
10. Walk On Campus At The University of Montana
11. The Garden Of 1000 Buddhas
12. Go Hiking On The Blue Mountain Trail
13. Hike To The 'M'
14. Go Floating On The River

15. Swim At Council Grove State Park
16. Get Dinner At The Montana Club Restaurant
17. Try The Hoagieville Cheese Fries
18. Get A Coffee At A Missoula Coffee Shop
19. Go To The Movies
20. See The Wilma Theater
21. Go Fishing
22. Go Rafting
23. Go To The Library To Read Up On Montana History
24. Shop At The Mall
25. Go Horse Back Riding Or Visit A Horse Show
26. Volunteer
27. Check Out Reserve Street
28. Hike To The L
29. Take Your Kids To Dragon Hollow
30. Garnet Ghost Town
31. Learn The History At Fort Missoula Museum
32. Walk The River Trail
33. Swim At Splash Montana
34. Ski At Montana Snowbowl
35. Drink Beers At A Montana Brewery
36. Hike At Pattee Canyon
37. Do A Wine Tasting At Ten Spoon Vineyard And Winery
38. See A Play At Missoula Children's Theater

39. See A Film At The Roxy
40. Take Your Dog to Jacob Island Dog Park
41. See The Beautiful Greenough Park
42. Try To Escape At Big Sky Breakout
43. Take A River City Brews River And Beer Tour
44. Shop At Missoula's Favorite Local Store: Rockin' Rudy's
45. Take Your Children to Flying Squirrel
46. Spend The Night Checking Out Missoula's Best Bars
47. Go Golfing At Canyon River Golf Club
48. Go Mountain-Biking Or Build A Bike At Free Cycles
49. Take Your Kids to The Hub
50. Move To Missoula

TOP REASONS TO BOOK THIS TRIP

Did you Know?

Other Resources:

TRIVIA

ANSWERS

Packing and Planning Tips

Travel Questions

Travel Bucket List

NOTES

DEDICATION

This book is dedicated to Kurt Rehder, my father, and the man who first showed me the beauty of Montana.

ABOUT THE AUTHOR

Ella Rehder is a freelance writer and editor that lives in Missoula, in the Big Sky state of Montana, USA. She grew up playing in the rivers, watching the infamous Montana sunsets, and fishing with her dad. Ella wanted to bring the inside scoop on Montana and its beauties—the open sky, the crystal-clear lakes, the beautiful birds that can be seen on a dewy Sunday morning, and the exciting feeling of playing with your dog in Missoula's dog park in the summer.

Ella lives with her dog, Ayla, and works from home during the pandemic. Her hobbies include writing poetry, singing, and creating new baking recipes. She also enjoys exploring Montana and writing about her discoveries. She is a published poet and experienced editor and hopes to publish non-fiction works in the future.

HOW TO USE THIS BOOK

The *Greater Than a Tourist* book series was written by someone who has lived in an area for over three months. The goal of this book is to help travelers either dream or experience different locations by providing opinions from a local. The author has made suggestions based on their own experiences. Please check before traveling to the area in case the suggested places are unavailable.

Travel Advisories: As a first step in planning any trip abroad, check the Travel Advisories for your intended destination.
https://travel.state.gov/content/travel/en/traveladvisories/traveladvisories.html

FROM THE PUBLISHER

Traveling can be one of the most important parts of a person's life. The anticipation and memories that you have are some of the best. As a publisher of the Greater Than a Tourist, as well as the popular *50 Things to Know* book series, we strive to help you learn about new places, spark your imagination, and inspire you. Wherever you are and whatever you do I wish you safe, fun, and inspiring travel.

Lisa Rusczyk Ed. D.
CZYK Publishing

>TOURIST

WELCOME TO
> TOURIST

>TOURIST

*University (Main) Hall, University of
Montana, in Missoula, Montana, United states.*

*view of Mount Sentinel from Higgins Bridge
in Missoula*

Missoula's Higgins Block

Terminal at Missoula International Airport, Montana, USA

>TOURIST

"I'm in love with Montana. For other states I have admiration, respect, recognition, even some affection. But with Montana, it is love. And it's difficult to analyze love when you're in it."

- John Steinbeck.

Montana is characterized by its large blue skies, beautiful white winters, outdoor sports, and the charm of the people. For this, it is called the Big Sky state. A state with a backdrop of blue, and gorgeous sunsets. You will feel like you're in paradise when you first see the starry night sky from a Montana campsite. In the west part of the state lies a small city called Missoula, a place where art, community, the outdoors, and music have come together to create a charming town that really shows what it means to be a Montanan.

Missoula, Montana is a unique and special destination. Some people believe that it does not even exist, as the few people who are lucky enough to be there are the people who are born there or people who know someone who lives there. Missoula is a small town, that feels like a small city. I am here to share its secrets with you today, from the best hiking spots to the best breweries, from the children's activities to activities you can do with your partner. With this guide of 50 things to know about Missoula, you will feel like a local by the time you put down this book.

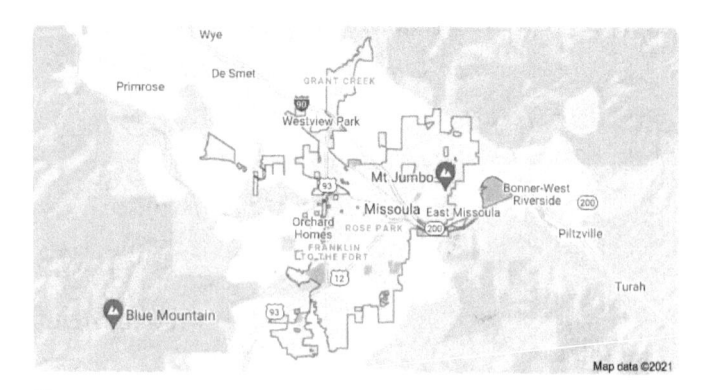

Missoula
Montana, USA

Missoula Montana Climate

	High	Low
January	34	19
February	40	23
March	49	28
April	57	34
May	66	41
June	74	47
July	85	52
August	84	51
September	73	43
October	58	34
November	42	26
December	33	19

GreaterThanaTourist.com

Temperatures are in Fahrenheit degrees.
Source: NOAA

>TOURIST

1. WATCH THE RIVER SURFERS AT CARAS PARK

Take a walk down to Caras Park to watch the river surfers. Next to Caras Park is the infamous Clarkfork River of Montana. It is a long and winding river that cuts right through the heart of downtown Missoula. Caras Park is a beautiful and family-friendly park that every local enjoys and knows. In the middle of Caras Park, on the Northside of Higgins Bridge is a small area next to a gigantic white tent. To the right of that is the popular river trail walking path. There is a wooden balcony that looks over the edge of the river there. Over the balcony, you can find the part of the Clarkfork where all our river surfers like to spend their mornings. You will see them out there every day, sometimes even in the colder seasons. I suggest going there in the summer. If you are someone who enjoys outdoor recreation and knows how to kayak, you could even join in and learn how to river surf yourself. Missoula has a river surfer's club, and you can investigate this online for more information.

2. TAKE A WALK DOWN TO BIG DIPPER ICE CREAM FOR A REFRESHING TREAT

Big Dipper Ice Cream has been featured in articles and travel blogs across the country as a must-go location in Montana. We have several across the state now, and almost every local in Missoula has taken a night trip to Big Dipper after a special event for a frozen treat. Their ice cream is creamy and delicious, and they have many flavors to choose from including bubblegum, vanilla, strawberry, cupcake, and the notorious huckleberry, a staple of being a Montanan. I recommend purchasing the waffle cone with huckleberry ice cream. Or you can try one of their famous huckleberry milkshakes. Go here in the summer evenings for a special Missoula experience you'll never forget.

3. RIDE 'A CAROUSEL FOR MISSOULA'

A Carousel For Missoula is another one of the most popular attractions in Missoula. You do not want to miss out on this opportunity, especially if you have young kids with you. I remember riding the carousel myself when I was a kid. I begged my parents every weekend to take us. The Carousel has a

>TOURIST

bunch of hand-painted and hand-carved horses and other animals to ride on. Missoula artists spend months working on the horses before adding them to the carousel. The art is some of the most beautiful I have seen. Some of the horses that were there when I was a child are still there today, and that was over 10 years ago! The best part of visiting the Carousel is that it is located directly in Caras Park, downtown. You can spend the day walking downtown or on the river trail and then head over to the carousel for some family-friendly fun.

4. TAKE A WALK IN THE HISTORIC DOWNTOWN DISTRICT

You have not really seen Missoula if you don't stop downtown for a walk. The downtown streets are beautiful at all times of the year. In the winter, the streets are lined with beautiful Christmas lights and wreaths, and all the shop lights illuminate the snow outside. Walking through the snow at night with the colored lights illuminating the way feels like your own personal winter wonderland. In the summer people walk around with their dogs and smile and chat in the streets. The coffee shops and restaurants have outdoor seating, and the locals are all happy to help you around. There are also many beautiful spots around town for photography opportunities.

Missoula is a very safe city, so you can feel safe talking to almost anyone and getting familiar with the stores and employees here. Stop by The Import Market for some unique gifts. Another good place to go is Liquid Planet, which is a coffee shop chain in Missoula. They have excellent coffees and some baked goods to try as well. You can spend an entire day downtown, with plenty to look at and experience. The shopping here is excellent and there is a wide variety of stores to peruse. This is a 10/10 experience for families, couples, and solo travelers alike.

5. VISIT THE SATURDAY FARMER'S MARKET

The Farmer's Market has always been one of my favorite parts of living in Missoula since I was a child. Every Saturday the main streets of downtown are closed for the market. Local vendors and artists set up their tables and stands for all of Missoula to come and shop and to see their art.

A section of the market is dedicated to fresh produce and food products. Some of the food I have seen sold here includes honey, homemade pickles, sauces, artisanal oils, bread, vegan cheeses, and ethically sourced meats. You can find almost any type of vegetable and fruit from one of our local farms here. All the vendors have reasonable prices for such delicious and organic food.

The other section of the market is dedicated to art, products, jewelry, and handmade products. You will find unique art such as magnets, paintings, handmade jewelry made from silverware, wood carvings, and metal sculptures.

To rent a table in Missoula for your business is very cheap, and all you must do is speak to the organizer of the market to reserve a spot. You can rent a table for the entire season or just for one day, it is your choice. They are only looking for people who sell handmade goods or own a small business.

Visiting the market is a great way for you to support Missoula locals and farms and meet new people. The market has been going strong since I was born. With the pandemic going on, the market has been smaller, but it will be back stronger than ever once it is safe again. This another great option for families and couples who are looking for a good way to live the authentic Missoulian experience.

6. EAT BREAKFAST AT THE CATALYST CAFÉ

The Catalyst is a small café in downtown Missoula that serves breakfast, brunch, and lunch. They also offer pre-made holiday meals during the pandemic for families. This café is locally owned and my favorite thing about them is that they value their employees and customers and treat them like family. You will have to come early to get a seat at this restaurant, as it is one of the most popular spots for breakfast in all of Missoula. I personally recommend their caramel latte if you're a big coffee drinker. They offer options for people with any taste. Their potato casserole is one of the more popular options. Their breakfasts are very affordable, and the staff is excellent. You can choose to sit upstairs or downstairs on the less busy days, or you can opt for outdoor seating in the hotter months. Overall, this is a great place to get breakfast before spending a day seeing the sights or walking around downtown.

7. GO HIKING IN THE RATTLESNAKE NATIONAL RECREATION AREA & WILDERNESS

Many trailheads lead to the Rattlesnake National Recreation Area & Wilderness. My personal favorite is Sawmill Gulch, which is down a winding road in the Rattlesnake neighborhood. The trail is alongside Rattlesnake Creek and is a great place to walk your dog. You can even ride horses in some parts of this trail. There are large moss-covered trees, small streams and brooks, level paths, and beautiful and long native grasses. You can walk down to the creek and wade on a hot day, or just sit and watch the water and reflect. This is not a particularly difficult hike, but there are a variety of other trails with varying

>TOURIST

difficulties in this area that you can find on Google Maps.

The Rattlesnake forest is one of the most beautiful nature spots in Missoula, and it is only a 10-minute drive from downtown. You can also find a variety of wildlife here including deer, birds, insects, frogs, and squirrels. Be careful in this area, as brown and black bears do live in the area. It is always good practice to bring bear spray or a loud bell to stay safe while walking.

This area is a wonderful area for recreational activities. I suggest flyfishing, hiking, horseback riding, birdwatching, foraging, or just sitting by the water and reading a book. I spent a lot of time here painting and reflecting. You can also camp in some areas. Make sure to research and find legal camping spots. You can get in trouble otherwise.

8. WATCH THE MONTANA SUNSET

The sunset in Missoula is one of the most beautiful I have seen. I have been to many states and even different countries, and the most beautiful sunset I ever saw was in Missoula. Not every sunset is like this, but sometimes the light hits just right and the sky turns different shades of pink, orange, and pastel colors. It looks like a painting or like a sorbet ice cream exploded in the sky. When the possibility arises, you can pull out some lawn chairs and sit outside and watch the beauty of our sunset. You can also lounge in Caras Park in the evening in the grass and watch from there. I suggest doing this in the summer when it is warm enough to enjoy it. Another option is to drive up to the South hills neighborhood to watch the sunset from your car in the highest-elevation residential neighborhood in the city.

9. VISIT THE ART MUSEUM OR AN ART GALLERY

Missoula is the place to be for artists in Montana. Our town is considered the "art capital," because of our local artists and the University of Montana, which has a large number of art students. You can also see some of the local art on the walls downtown. We have a variety of art stores and galleries downtown. The Missoula Art Museum also lives downtown and is home to many exhibits. They host events for local groups and schools as well. I have been to art showings, reward events, poetry readings, and school events here. Any art enthusiast will feel at home here. You can even buy art from most of these places. We have a new art gallery open now called Radius. You can also check out the Dana Gallery or The Artist's Shop. Both have art you can buy and look at. Both galleries host local artists, including up-and-coming artists that are less known. Some of my friends have had their work shown here. The Dana Gallery hosts a poetry reading from one of the local high schools yearly.

10. WALK ON CAMPUS AT THE UNIVERSITY OF MONTANA

The University of Montana is one of the most known parts of Missoula and Montana in general. Out of town visitors tend to be University students or families of students there. The campus of The University of Montana is gorgeous and is a must-see when you are visiting. In the fall the large Maple trees here turn bright orange, red, and pink. You can walk through the fallen leaves with a hot coffee and enjoy the sights at the University. The University also has a grocery store, a bookstore, and the famous Food Zoo cafeteria which has buffet-style meals for cheap. Even if you're not a student you can go here for meals if you are with a student or faculty of the school. The buildings at the University are historic and beautiful, made from red brick. The buildings were built as early as 1893 and many are still the original building. The University takes great pride in restoring its buildings and keeping the historic look. Take photos with the clock tower in the middle of campus and see what Missoula's students get to experience every day.

For people who are looking to attend school here, you can apply online or pay a visit to the registrar's office on campus. It is possible to apply to live on campus in one of the many dormitory buildings as well. I lived in Knowles hall when I attended, and it was great. The University staff are kind and welcoming to all new students. The campus hosts many events for a large variety of topics. Since this is considered an art and music school, the campus is LGBTQ+ friendly and supportive of students of color and other minorities. They also host international exchange students from several countries. The University is a welcoming environment in a small city, which allows students to study in the day and spend time in nature in their free time. I strongly suggest this if you are someone who loves nature, hiking, silence, and freedom.

11. THE GARDEN OF 1000 BUDDHAS

This location is about 30 miles away from Missoula, but I still consider it a must-see spot, even if you are not religious or have a different religion. The garden was built along with 1000 statues of Buddha and it is a place for reflection, spirituality, growth, and experiencing nature. The garden hosts events and offers volunteer opportunities, even if you are just visiting. In the spring the garden has beautiful and colorful flowers growing all around and a pond with fish. You can sit at the pond and watch the fish and reflect. I used to go here and draw.

The Garden of 1000 Buddhas is in Arlee, Montana, which is on the Native American

>TOURIST

reservation. Take a right turn off the highway onto White Coyote Lane to find this spot. This spot is not known by everyone, so there are often not many people here. All they ask of you is to be respectful, do not throw your trash on the ground, do not bring pets, and come with a peaceful attitude. There is handicapped parking closer to the path if you need it, and a parking lot inside the main gate. Staff always work and live in the garden. On the weekdays their small store is open. The gift shop sells Buddhist garments, snacks, sodas, books, and other souvenirs. There are chances to also learn about the history of the garden by speaking to the cashier or purchasing a book about it there. There is an extensive and interesting story behind it all.

Donating money to the garden is possible, in exchange for a plaque on one of their statues, or as a standalone donation. For the plaque option, you can dedicate your statue to people who have died or anyone in your life that you want to pay homage to. The money goes to maintaining the plants, grass, pond, and land that the garden sits on, as well as events and volunteer opportunities. I have heard that people have even been able to put ashes or special items inside the small statue when they purchase the plaque. This is a meaningful and peaceful place to go, and I strongly suggest it if you're interested.

12. GO HIKING ON THE BLUE MOUNTAIN TRAIL

This is another tip for those that love to hike and be outdoors. Missoula has many beautiful trails, and this is one of my favorites. Blue Mountain trail is less forest-y and more of a field and view type of hike. You hike up a beautiful hill of long native grasses and at the top, you can look over the hill and see Missoula. In the spring there are natural wildflowers that dot the hills. Blue Mountain is also a great spot to take your dog if you're looking to bring your furry friend.

13. HIKE TO THE 'M'

One of the most famous landmarks in Missoula is the 'M' mountain. On top of Mount Sentinel is a large M made from concrete. You can see it from the moment you drive into Missoula, and from most places in Missoula. The M is also a hiking trail. Almost every Missoulian I know has hiked to it. You start at the base, behind the University campus, and you walk up the steep trail until you reach the top. At the top of the mountain, you can see the entire city, from downtown to Reserve St. The hike isn't terribly difficult, but you might get a bit tired if you're not used to treks like this. The trail is frequently walked and safe. You can hike The M at any time, which

>TOURIST

means you can go at night if you wish and see all the lights of Missoula from above when there aren't as many people. This is a very beautiful experience, and I recommend it.

14. GO FLOATING ON THE RIVER

In the summer, it is a well-known Missoula tradition for everyone to go floating on the river. This means going to one of our local river shops and buying some inner tubes and heading out to the river for a day of floating and fun. You can even hire a river shuttle to drop you off and pick you up at the end of your float. They also offer the option to rent inflatable kayaks or inner tubes from them for the day if you don't want to buy them. Taking their shuttles to the river is an easier option if you don't want to deal with the hassle and organization of parking in two locations. There are even some that are free. Just make sure you schedule ahead of time.

Floating may seem scary and dangerous, but if you know the correct spots, you'll be okay. I suggest the float from Kelly Island to Kona Bridge. This route about an hour or two and it's relatively safe. You can stop on the shore for lunch. There weren't as many people on this route as you might see on the downtown route through the Clarkfork river and East Missoula.

You can buy sealed bags to put your drinks and food in and dangle it in the water to keep them cold. The river is very cold, but this is part of the Montana experience. With the summer heat sometimes reaching over 100 degrees, you'll be happy to take a swim in the freezing water.

15. SWIM AT COUNCIL GROVE STATE PARK

My favorite swimming area in the summer is Council Grove State Park. The road to the trail might be a little bit tricky to find. You need to drive down Mullan Rd. until you find a fishing access sign. You'll turn left at that sign instead of following the GPS. Once there, you can park in the parking area.

To get to the swimming spot, you'll take a quick walk down a dirt trail and then you'll reach the beach area. Here you can swim because the water is slow, less dangerous, and very deep. This part of the river is also very cold. If you go in the summer, it won't be a problem. You can bring your kids and pets here as well.

>TOURIST

16. GET DINNER AT THE MONTANA CLUB RESTAURANT

The Montana Club is one of my favorite restaurants for lunch or dinner. They have rustic-style and Montana-inspired décor in both of their restaurants. They serve steaks, pasta, and some of the biggest Nachos I've ever seen. My favorite meal there is their Garlic Button Sirloin steak.

The Montana Club also is present in a couple of other Montana towns, as it has become a Montana favorite food chain. This is a good spot for family dining, but you can also have a romantic dinner here if you choose. This restaurant is not a fine dining experience but is a bit more expensive than other restaurants in Missoula.

17. TRY THE HOAGIEVILLE CHEESE FRIES

Hoagieville is a Montana food chain fast-food restaurant that started in Missoula. Unlike other fast-food chains, they were created by locals and have delicious homemade recipes. I've been eating there since I was a kid. Hoagieville is home to the best fry seasoning in the world. You must try it. Go there and order the Hoagie Cheese Fries and see what all the hype is about. You can also buy their famous fry seasoning in a bottle to take home and make your own fries.

18. GET A COFFEE AT A MISSOULA COFFEE SHOP

Missoula is home to many local coffee shops. We also have Starbucks, but if you're looking for a local business to support, there are plenty. One of the bigger and more popular chains of coffee stores is City Brew. There are three or four in Missoula. We also have Liquid Planet, which is probably the most popular. They have one downtown, one in the airport, one in the courthouse, one outside of Lowe's, and a few others scattered around.

Florence Coffee Company is another good choice. There are many drive-up coffee stands in Missoula and some other Montana towns where you can get their well-known invigorating coffees. They add more espresso to their coffee than most other places, and their flavoring is to die for. I always order a caramel breve here. At all these places you can try the huckleberry flavoring in your drink. They all sell baked goods and snacks as well. Try some Montana-style snacks and drinks or make a quick Google Maps search to find more local coffee shops.

>TOURIST

19. GO TO THE MOVIES

Missoula is now home to two movie theaters. One of them is a dine-in theater, which allows you to eat dinner while you watch your film. Although you can go to the movie in any state, Missoula's movie experience is different. There aren't a lot of people in Missoula, so often you will get to go to the movies alone and enjoy the movie yourself. During the Covid-19 pandemic, the dine-in theater is offering disposable dishes and cups for your food and is seating people 4 seats apart. The staff here are always friendly and welcoming. Have a fun family night out and see the movies! On Tuesdays, tickets are five dollars each.

20. SEE THE WILMA THEATER

The Wilma is one of Missoula's oldest buildings, and it sits downtown right before the Higgins St. Bridge. The building is still the original, and you can see it in old pictures of downtown Missoula from the early 1900s. Even today, The Wilma still hosts performances. I even went to my senior prom there. In October, they host the yearly performance of Rocky Horror, which is put on by University students and actors in the community. This theater is a must-see and a beautiful historic building. Sometimes you can rent out rooms on the top floors of the building, where there are apartments and offices. You can find these rooms on Airbnb or look them up on Google. See Missoula from the center of downtown. You'll find that this will be a once-in-a-lifetime experience. Look online to see when The Wilma will host their next event or concert. There is a possibility that it might be while you're there.

21. GO FISHING

Missoula is also a great hub for fishing. A lot of people travel here for fishing opportunities. We have a large amount of rainbow trout, which are delicious when grilled. Fly fishing is also common here. You can find fish bait just about anywhere, and there are several fishing and hunting stores around Missoula. You can find live bait at some convenience stores, especially the ones close to the rivers in the smaller towns outside of Missoula, like Alberton.

I also suggest watching the movie, "A River Runs Through It," which is set in Missoula. The movie is about fly fishing and the beauty of Montana nature. Anyone who has an interest in this will love the movie.

>TOURIST

22. GO RAFTING

Even if you don't know how to raft or do not own a raft, it's as simple as walking down to the closest river shop and renting one. You can also sign up for guided raft tours and rafting classes at these shops. For people who are a bit nervous about navigating the river in a raft, get a guide who can take you to the safest spots and show you the ropes.

For more experienced rafters looking for a once-in-a-lifetime rafting experience, go to Alberton Gorge. You've probably heard of it if you're an avid rafter. The water here is extremely dangerous, so wear life-vests. People who are not experienced rafters should not try this. People have been known to flip their rafts in the water here. For those who enjoy extreme water activities, this might be up your alley. Just make sure you research it extensively before going. There are guided raft tours here as well. Alberton is about a 40-minute drive out of Missoula.

23. GO TO THE LIBRARY TO READ UP ON MONTANA HISTORY

For all the history lovers like I am, you'll enjoy knowing that Missoula Public Library has an entire section dedicated to the history of Missoula and Montana in general. They have saved hundreds of records of newspapers, journals, and more from the early 1900s in Missoula. You can take these journals and view them up close in their own viewing software. For people who are looking for records about someone in your family that lived in this area, or records about buildings in Missoula, this is a great place to find it. The librarians here will also be more than helpful in assisting you with the equipment.

I also suggest going to the library for regular reading. Recently the library was upgraded into a bigger building that is still near the old location. The building will have large modern glass windows and a café and will house more books and more learning areas. They will be able to host more events. After the pandemic, I suggest going to the library for events and classes as well. You can also check out books.

>TOURIST

24. SHOP AT THE MALL

Southgate Mall is Missoula's only shopping mall. Although it may seem small, it hosts a lot of local businesses. If you're looking to support some local shops while also shopping at bigger chains like H&M and Victoria Secret, then this is the place to go. You can find four department stores here as well. Southgate Mall is always changing and improving, so there are always events or new things to see inside.

Around the holidays, Southgate Mall hosts photos with Santa, Halloween parties, Halloween trick-or-treat at all the stores, and more. Sometimes during the year, they'll have events for adults too, where you can buy alcohol and enter giveaways for store gift cards. There are many competitions, music performances, and art galleries that are put up throughout the mall during the year. The mall also likes to host the artwork of children from local schools. During the school year, you'll see the art hung up and pinned to walls for you to look at.

I think the mall is unique to other malls in bigger places because it's very localized. You will find many Missoula-specific displays and photos throughout the mall. To get to the bathroom, you walk through a hallway with historic photography of Missoula when it began. Take a minute to look through it all if you'd like to see a better image in your head of what Missoula has grown from.

25. GO HORSE BACK RIDING OR VISIT A HORSE SHOW

Many of Missoula's residents are local farmers or ranchers. There are many opportunities in town to experience farm life. If you look online, you can find opportunities for guided trail riding. Missoula is home to many trails that allow horses, so you can see some beautiful scenery while on the back of a horse. Check out the local ranches online to find out more about this option.

If you're an equestrian at heart, you might also enjoy visiting a horse show. We have an equestrian park in the Orchard Homes area of town. They host jumping, Western and English confirmation, and more. You can come and watch it any time. Just check their schedules online.

26. VOLUNTEER

You can find many volunteer opportunities in Missoula. The heart of Missoula, in my opinion, is the people. Everyone here wants to help the community and make it a better place to live for everyone. We have a large population of homeless people and families. Missoula has several organizations that work to end poverty and hunger in our community.

One of these organizations is The Poverello, which is our homeless shelter. You can volunteer here at any

>TOURIST

time to offer food, support, or staffing to the shelter and the people there. You can also serve our homeless and poor population by volunteering at our local Missoula Food Bank. Both The Poverello and the Food Bank have newly renovated buildings, made possible by donations from people in the community. Missoula is looking to create another homeless shelter in the future.

If you're looking to volunteer in other ways, you can volunteer labor to local gardens and co-ops, or you can volunteer your time at the Public Library. A lot of our local businesses look for volunteers. Search for "volunteering in Missoula" online and you'll find more opportunities not listed here.

27. CHECK OUT RESERVE STREET

For people looking for retail shopping and the heart of corporate Missoula, Reserve St. is where to go. Along the street, we have most of our large chain stores and restaurants. You can find Walmart, Target, Starbucks, Rosauers, WinCo, Albertsons, Petco, and more. All the big stores tend to be bunched together, so you can find everything you're looking to buy in one trip. Even though these aren't local businesses, I know that sometimes it might be needed just need to go to Target for that one item you were looking for. Every town has stores like these, and this is where Missoula's are.

28. HIKE TO THE L

A bit lesser known, The L is another mountain hike in Missoula, to the left of The M., The L is the same as The M in many ways, except that it is less hiked. This concrete letter sits up on the top of Mount Jumbo. The letter represents Loyola Catholic High School, a Christian school in Missoula. You can hike up to this letter from the base. The trail is a trickier hike and not as worn, so you might have a harder time getting up. If you're an experienced hiker, you'll like this one. The trail is also less crowded than The M, so you can go and have some alone time if you're looking for it.

29. TAKE YOUR KIDS TO DRAGON HOLLOW

Right behind The Carousel for Missoula is a large wooden play structure created for children and families to enjoy. The wooden structure was built when I was a child, and my name is actually engraved on the fence, along with other children's names whose families donated to the park during its construction. Dragon's Hollow is not just a regular playground. What sets it apart is the size and its many corners and parts to explore. The park is fenced off from the rest of Caras Park, so you can be sure your children will be safe to run and play here. This is a great place to stop with your kids if you've spent the day walking the river trail and seeing Caras Park. Or you can play here after taking a ride on the carousel.

30. GARNET GHOST TOWN

Garnet Ghost Town is outside of Missoula. The drive takes about an hour from town. The road up to the parking area is a bit rough, so make sure you are used to dirt road driving and high-altitude locations. Check your tire pressure before going. There are many beautiful things to look at on the drive there. You can see some of Montana's rural culture.

Once you arrive at the ghost town, you'll see why it's such a popular destination. The town has been restored and opened as a museum. You can walk around the town just as if it was another city. You can enter most of the buildings and read history about them, as well as the people that lived inside.

The town also has a gift shop with books and souvenirs that will help you learn more about Garnet and why people settled there. Make sure you check their hours online and call ahead of time. Sometimes the town is closed for repairs or because of the weather. You most likely won't be able to make the drive up when there's a lot of snow on the ground. The best time of year to go is in the spring or the summer.

31. LEARN THE HISTORY AT FORT MISSOULA MUSEUM

Fort Missoula is a museum that was set up in the old historic buildings of Fort Missoula. The fort was used as a housing center for illegal immigrants in 1941 and 1944. Some of the sadder histories about this can be found on their website or placards in the museum.

During the pandemic, you can view the museum virtually on their website, or you can visit with a mask and social distancing guidelines, which you can also find on their website. The museum hosts many exhibits and things to look at, so start early and look at everything they've got to offer. You'll find out a lot about Missoula's history here. They've got information on the old railway systems as well. You can also learn the history of each building in the fort.

Outside of the museum campus, there are parks and recreation areas to play and eat lunch. You can also take your dogs to the new dog park that opened here. Sometimes in the summer, there are events held in the park areas. The Fort is always expanding and growing its resources and campus, so check their website to learn more.

>TOURIST

32. WALK THE RIVER TRAIL

I mentioned the river trail earlier in the book, but it deserves its own paragraph. The river trail is a large concrete trail that stretches around both sides of the river, connected by walking bridges. The trail is great for riding bikes, skateboarding, walking your dog, and family outings. Lots of people use the trail every day to get in their morning jog. Check it out on a warm day and see what all the hype is about.

33. SWIM AT SPLASH MONTANA

Near Sentinel High School is Missoula's waterpark, Splash Montana. With three large water slides, a lazy river, and an Olympic swimming pool, it is a wonderful spot to go with your family in the late spring and the summer months. The waterpark opens at the end of May and you can spend the day there swimming and enjoying the water in the heat. In the lazy river, they offer inner tubes for you to sit and enjoy the current while your kids play in the water. You can slide down the orange slide in a two-person inner tube. This can even be fun for adults. I go there in the summer too, and they have adult nights that you can find on their Facebook page as events. On adult night, you can drink wine and swim with friends without all the noise and splashing of children. The park has a café and an ice cream stand, so you can be sure you'll have a fun-filled day without interruption.

34. SKI AT MONTANA SNOWBOWL

For people who like to ski, Montana Snowbowl is a great choice. The Snowbowl is one of our most popular skiing areas and is open almost all times of the year. The location is a bit out of town, but if you're willing to make the drive, it is worth it. You will find slopes for beginners and experts here. Montana is great for skiing because there is snow on the mountain-tops year-round. You can stay in lodging resorts just outside and eat at restaurants there. This is another place that feels like a winter wonderland, and it is a great way to experience the outdoor sports of Montana.

35. DRINK BEERS AT A MONTANA BREWERY

Missoula is well-known for its breweries, as there are many. A lot of our local breweries have beer brands that you've probably never tried. Some of the most popular breweries include Bayern Brewery, Big Sky Brewing, and Montgomery Distillery. A lot of the breweries allow you to even look through the windows to the brewing process. If you're interested in how it works, just head on over to one of the most famous breweries and see it in action. Get a drink

>TOURIST

while you're there and see what Missoulians are drinking.

36. HIKE AT PATTEE CANYON

Another popular hiking area in Missoula is Pattee Canyon. There are many trails within this area, so just driving up the road and looking for one that looks promising for you is a good plan. You can also check out Google Maps. A lot of the trails in Pattee Canyon are steep and uphill, so if you're someone that likes the uphill climb, this is a good area for you. The trails go on for miles, and you can camp in some areas if you trek far enough. Be on the lookout for bears and mountain lions, like in most areas in the wilderness of Montana. You can bring your pets to these trails as well. Keep them on a leash unless specified otherwise.

37. DO A WINE TASTING AT TEN SPOON VINEYARD AND WINERY

Ten Spoon Vineyard and Winery is a winery in Missoula that offers Montana-made wines. You can go here for a wine-tasting event, or just explore the area and buy a bottle of wine from a Montana local business. The winery has great reviews and is highly recommended by wine enthusiasts. It is also a great place to go for a romantic date with your partner. You may not have thought of Montana as a hub for wine, but our wine is quite tasty. The locals are excellent at crafting artisanal alcoholic beverages.

38. SEE A PLAY AT MISSOULA CHILDREN'S THEATER

Despite the name, Missoula Children's Theater isn't just children. Many popular Broadway musicals are redone and performed here by actors, dancers, and musicians in Missoula. There are also children's performances done here by kids who have auditioned for roles in plays. You can find almost anything you're looking for here, just check their schedule online to see when the next performance is.

39. SEE A FILM AT THE ROXY

Like the Wilma, Roxy is another historic theater in Missoula. However, it is a bit smaller and is made for small performances and movies. The Roxy often shows older films and artistic films for people to come to watch. They sell concessions and have small theater rooms with movie theater-style chairs. I've also gone there to see comedy shows and presentations.

>TOURIST

The Roxy is popular among young people, especially university students. Just a few blocks from one of our high schools, and close to downtown, it's a great place to find other young people or to see a film with friends. The theater doesn't often offer children's movies. The Roxy is mostly an adult location. Date night here is always something special, and it's a Missoulian experience for sure.

40. TAKE YOUR DOG TO JACOB ISLAND DOG PARK

Missoula is home to my favorite dog park. I've traveled to many cities, and Missoula has the best one by far. Jacob's Island is a small island in the middle of the Clarkfork river. On the island is the dog park, which is a large fenced-in area for your dogs to run off-leash. The dog park leads back into many trails through the dunes on the island. You can explore the entire island with your dogs. It is also a popular stopping point for people floating the Clarkfork river, so you will often see people exiting the water here.

Your dogs can swim and meet other dogs at this park. On a warm day, there are usually about 10 to 20 dogs at the park. You don't have to worry about your dog getting lost, because the island is surrounded by water, and your dog will always be within the boundaries of the park. The only thing I suggest is making sure your dog is up to date on vaccinations and is socialized with other dogs. Some dogs at the park can be untrained and aggressive, so always be on watch, and have fun!

41. SEE THE BEAUTIFUL GREENOUGH PARK

To feel like a true Missoula native, you must see Greenough Park. The park is one of many in the Rattlesnake neighborhood. This small slice of paradise is nestled between a mountain and the Rattlesnake forest. Rattlesnake creek runs through the middle of it. Throughout the park, there are various grassy areas to have a picnic or rocky beaches where you can wade in the creek. I had my senior photos taken here, so I promise it's a beautiful area. You can bring your dogs and go for a jog, or you can just walk and see the surroundings. I suggest going here in the autumn when the leaves turn red and orange and pink. Greenough is beautiful and worth the visit. If you enjoy photography, this is a great spot for photos. Try taking some on the bridge entering the park, or in the autumn leaves when they fall on the ground. You won't regret it.

\>TOURIST

42. TRY TO ESCAPE AT BIG SKY BREAKOUT

Missoula now has its very own escape room with several rooms to try to break out of. For 25 dollars for adults, 15 dollars for children, and 20 dollars for students, elders, and the military. Their escape levels and rooms are always changing, so check out their website for information. This is a great opportunity for families with children.

43. TAKE A RIVER CITY BREWS RIVER AND BEER TOUR

River City Brews takes you on a river adventure on the Clarkfork where you and your friends or adult family can take a rafting tour on the river and try Missoula's local beers. You can choose your pick-up location and they will drive you to the rafting area. You can choose from beers or cider for your drinking experience as well. The river tour hosts up to 12 people. Book online or over the phone using their website information.

44. SHOP AT MISSOULA'S FAVORITE LOCAL STORE: ROCKIN' RUDY'S

Rockin' Rudy's is the best place to get presents, gag gifts, spiritual items, cards, gift bags, local Missoulian art, toys, handmade jewelry, and more. This store has just about anything you could think of for a gift shop. Rockin' Rudy's tries to fill as much of the store as possible with local business and artist merchandise. You can buy handmade clothes as well. The proceeds go towards the artists and the store, keeping Missoula a community that strives towards togetherness and art revival.

45. TAKE YOUR CHILDREN TO FLYING SQUIRREL

Flying Squirrel is a gymnastics center for children consisting of only a trampoline floor, with some foam pits and seating areas. Children can come here to jump on the trampolines until they get tired. They will be given special grip-socks when you pay for the experience so that they don't fall on the trampolines. There is a café and an arcade here as well. Your family is guaranteed to have a very fun time here.

>TOURIST

46. SPEND THE NIGHT CHECKING OUT MISSOULA'S BEST BARS

Downtown Missoula is home to many bars. If you're looking for the local nightlife experience, I'll give you the inside scoop. Bars that are popular with young University students are The Badlander and The Golden Rose. Both bars host live music from some of Missoula's local bands. The bars are connected through a hallway.

For older folks, Imagination Brewing and Western Cider are good options. Both bars host events as well. Imagination Brewing has its own beer brand and Western Cider sells alcoholic ciders, hence the name. At times, the bars have live music and other events. I went to a few poetry readings at Imagination Brewing.

The Top Hat and Thomas Meager Bar are good bars to go to for a drink and food. Thomas Meager hosts karaoke and has sports channels for watching sports with your friends. The Top Hat is more upscale and has higher-end dining and drinks. They host New Years' parties here and often have bigger local bands showcasing here. Both are great options if you're looking for a classy bar experience.

47. GO GOLFING AT CANYON RIVER GOLF CLUB

If you enjoy golfing, Missoula has its very own golf and country club. You can head there for some outdoor time with friends. Their course is something that will be pleasurable for any level player. If you're a golf newbie, you can still have fun here. If you're a pro, come see what it's like to golf in the beautiful Montana nature. The golf course also hosts a bar and restaurant for when you're tired after a long day of golfing.

48. GO MOUNTAIN-BIKING OR BUILD A BIKE AT FREE CYCLES

For people that enjoy biking in nature, Missoula is great for mountain biking. We have several bike shops if you're looking for a new mountain bike that will get you over those tough Montana trails. You can also opt for a free option and build your own bike at Free Cycles, a non-profit organization that takes donated bike parts and allows people to build bikes out of them for free. Consider donating to them as well, to allow them to keep their store open for more people to receive bikes for free.

>TOURIST

A good spot to mountain bike is in The Rattlesnake. Many trails allow mountain biking. I see a lot of mountain bikers on the Sawmill Gulch trails. You can also look online to see where other bikers like to go in Missoula.

49. TAKE YOUR KIDS TO THE HUB

The Hub is a large arcade and entertainment zone for children and families. Inside is a large arcade with lots of prizes, a bumper cars track, and laser tag. If you're looking for another indoor spot for children, this is it. The Hub also has a café for when you're done playing. This is a great place for all-day fun with your children.

50. MOVE TO MISSOULA

Do you want to see Missoula through the eyes of a local? If so, you can follow all the tips above, but you could also consider moving here. Missoula is a beautiful and diverse city in many ways. The locals are friendly and peaceful, and we strive to keep a sense of community. If you're the kind of person who is looking for an artistic town and you want to add to the community, Missoula will feel like home the second you step into it. You will find that

Missoulians take pride in our city and the beauty in the nature around us. You can wake up each day to take a 10-minute hike into the forest or to watch the sunrise over the river. You can write in the woods or paint the scenery with a delicious Missoula beer in hand. If you're looking for extreme outdoor sports, we have that too.

Missoula is a wonderful place to live, although a bit expensive. As the city expands, there is more and more to see each day. There will be more being built right now that I can't even put in this guide, because it's not here yet. If you're looking for an expanding city with potential, but with the feel of a small town, this place will fulfill your dreams.

So, converse with one of our property management companies to find a home that fits your style. You can also talk to one of the many real estate companies downtown for information on Montana houses for sale. There are limitless possibilities in the Big Sky state. Come see what Missoula is about. Get the local perspective as a local.

>TOURIST

TOP REASONS TO BOOK THIS TRIP

Outdoor Sports: Missoula hosts rafting, river surfing, mountain biking, hunting, fishing, and more. You can find information about this through our many outdoor sports companies online.

River Culture: Missoula is located between two rivers—the Clarkfork and the Bitterroot. Both rivers offer great opportunities for swimming, fishing, water sports, and floating.

Hiking Opportunities: There are many trailheads in Missoula; I think there are too many to count. Hikers and outdoor enthusiasts love Missoula's natural beauty and camping opportunities.

Art: Missoula is Montana's art capital. You can find many spots that host art galleries. You can even create your own art here at places like "Painting with a Twist."

Music: Our city also hosts concerts and music events. We have our own local bands, but also host bands from out of state. Some bigger bands I've seen in Missoula are The Fray, Brandi Carlisle, and LP. Our music venues are some of the best in the country. You can buy tickets to concerts at Rockin' Rudy's.

Locals: The locals are the best thing about Missoula because without us there wouldn't be a sense of community and a love for the arts. The Missoulians keep the town together.

>TOURIST

DID YOU KNOW?

-Missoula sits in a canyon. It used to be entirely underwater. The valley was carved out by the water and is now home to the Montana city.

-Before Missoula, the land was home to several Native American tribes. Those tribes now live in reservations further up, like the reservation in Arlee, but it's good to remember the history of the land. You can find out more information about the Native history here through the Native American Center at The University of Montana.

-Lewis & Clark passed through Missoula on their journey. You can find out more about this at Missoula's Lewis & Clark center, and the monument put up outside the river right before Easy St. in East Missoula.

-Wildlife is something you must get used to here. Deer are everywhere in the streets at all times of the day. Make sure you're watching out for deer when you drive through the residential areas especially. Take bear spray on hikes and watch out for mountain lions in the more reserved areas. Make sure you know how to protect yourself.

-Missoula's temperatures go from extremes such as -10 degrees in the winter to 105 degrees in the summer. The climate here is very dry, so it feels very harsh at times.

-Glacier National Park is just a few hours' drive from Missoula.

-Yellowstone Park is also fairly close, and you can take a weekend trip there from Missoula by car.

-The largest seen snowflake fell in Missoula in 1887. It was 15 inches wide.

-Jeannette Rankin was the first woman in the U.S elected to Congress. She was from Missoula.

-The University of Montana has a football team called The Grizzlies

-Local teenagers like to dive into the rivers off bridges

-Missoula is very safe. You can feel safe leaving your laptop out when you go to the bathroom in a public place. This is different than in bigger cities.

-Missoula is a host to the International Choral Festival.

-There are more deer and elk in Montana than people.

-Flathead lake is one of the clearest lakes in the country.

-You can buy inner tubes for floating outside the local Albertsons in the summer.

-You can buy fresh huckleberries at the Farmer's market for pies or for eating.

>TOURIST

OTHER RESOURCES:

www.airbnb.com – Airbnb has several Missoula rentals that you can stay in for up to a few months to see the area. You can stay in log cabins, apartments in the heart of downtown, or family homes. Many are equipped with bathrooms, kitchens, bedrooms, living rooms, yards, and more. This is a cheaper alternative to a hotel.

www.uber.com – Missoula is home to Uber, the famous ride-sharing app. We also have Lyft. If you're here without a car and need a quick ride, Uber is a great choice.

https://montanariverguides.com/ - If you're looking for river tours or rafting guides, this website has information on Missoula's river scene.

www.destinationmissoula.org – This website has tons of travel information for tourists. It has information on topics such as food and drink, sights to see, housing, and Montana history. This is a must-see guide if you'd like more information after reading mine.

St. Patrick's Hospital – 4065437271
Missoula Police Department – 4062584810
Missoula Airport Shuttle- 4068807433
Destination Missoula- 4065323250

www.fortmissoulamuseum.org – Information on Fort Missoula and Missoula history.

www.missoulapubliclibrary.org – Missoula's library and center for history.

www.umt.edu – University of Montana website.

www.ci.missoula.mt.us/2400/help-lines-and-local-resources - A guide for local resources and helplines.

Destination Missoula Welcome Center- 101 E Main St, Missoula, MT 59802

>TOURIST

TRIVIA

1) What is the name of the two main rivers in Missoula?

2) What neighborhood in Missoula is the Wilma theater located in?

3) How many miles is it to drive from the Rattlesnake to Reserve St.?

4) What famous people were born in Missoula?

5) When was Missoula settled?

6) What famous movie was set in Missoula?

7) What towns frame the outskirts of Missoula?

8) What are the names of the three high schools in town?

9) When was the University of Montana founded?

10) When was Missoula founded?

ANSWERS

1) Clarkfork & Bitterroot
2) Downtown
3) 6 miles
4) David Lynch, Jeanette Rankin, Jesse Tyler Ferguson, Dana Carvey, Eden Atwood, Harold Urey, Brian Schmidt
5) 1806
6) A River Runs Through It
7) Frenchtown, East Missoula, Clinton, Stevensville, Lolo
8) Hellgate, Sentinel, and Big Sky
9) 1893
10) 1864

\>TOURIST

PACKING AND PLANNING TIPS

A Week before Leaving

- Arrange for someone to take care of pets and water plants.
- Email and Print important Documents.
- Get Visa and vaccines if needed.
- Check for travel warnings.
- Stop mail and newspaper.
- Notify Credit Card companies where you are going.
- Passports and photo identification is up to date.
- Pay bills.
- Copy important items and download travel Apps.
- Start collecting small bills for tips.
- Have post office hold mail while you are away.
- Check weather for the week.
- Car inspected, oil is changed, and tires have the correct pressure.
- Check airline luggage restrictions.
- Download Apps needed for your trip.

Right Before Leaving

- Contact bank and credit cards to tell them your location.
- Clean out refrigerator.
- Empty garbage cans.
- Lock windows.
- Make sure you have the proper identification with you.
- Bring cash for tips.
- Remember travel documents.
- Lock door behind you.
- Remember wallet.
- Unplug items in house and pack chargers.
- Change your thermostat settings.
- Charge electronics, and prepare camera memory cards.

\>TOURIST

READ OTHER GREATER THAN A TOURIST BOOKS

Greater Than a Tourist- California: 50 Travel Tips from Locals

Greater Than a Tourist- Salem Massachusetts USA 50 Travel Tips from a Local by Danielle Lasher

Greater Than a Tourist United States: 50 Travel Tips from Locals

Greater Than a Tourist- St. Croix US Birgin Islands USA: 50 Travel Tips from a Local by Tracy Birdsall

Greater Than a Tourist- Montana: 50 Travel Tips from a Local by Laurie White

Children's Book: Charlie the Cavalier Travels the World by Lisa Rusczyk Ed. D.

> TOURIST

Follow us on Instagram for beautiful travel images:
http://Instagram.com/GreaterThanATourist

Follow *Greater Than a Tourist* on Amazon.

CZYKPublishing.com

> TOURIST

At *Greater Than a Tourist*, we love to share travel tips with you. How did we do? What guidance do you have for how we can give you better advice for your next trip? Please send your feedback to GreaterThanaTourist@gmail.com as we continue to improve the series. We appreciate your constructive feedback. Thank you.

> TOURIST

METRIC CONVERSIONS

TEMPERATURE

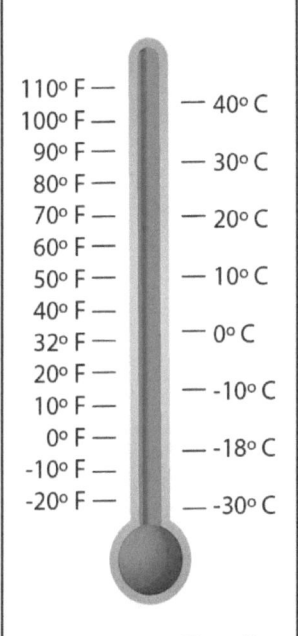

- 110° F — 40° C
- 100° F
- 90° F — 30° C
- 80° F
- 70° F — 20° C
- 60° F
- 50° F — 10° C
- 40° F
- 32° F — 0° C
- 20° F
- 10° F — -10° C
- 0° F
- -10° F — -18° C
- -20° F — -30° C

To convert F to C:
Subtract 32, and then multiply by 5/9 or .5555.

To Convert C to F:
Multiply by 1.8 and then add 32.

32F = 0C

LIQUID VOLUME

To Convert:	Multiply by
U.S. Gallons to Liters	3.8
U.S. Liters to Gallons	26
Imperial Gallons to U.S. Gallons	1.2
Imperial Gallons to Liters	4.55
Liters to Imperial Gallons	22

1 Liter = .26 U.S. Gallon
1 U.S. Gallon = 3.8 Liters

DISTANCE

To convert	Multiply by
Inches to Centimeters	2.54
Centimeters to Inches	39
Feet to Meters	.3
Meters to Feet	3.28
Yards to Meters	91
Meters to Yards	1.09
Miles to Kilometers	1.61
Kilometers to Miles	.62

1 Mile = 1.6 km
1 km = .62 Miles

WEIGHT

1 Ounce = .28 Grams
1 Pound = .4555 Kilograms
1 Gram = .04 Ounce
1 Kilogram = 2.2 Pounds

>TOURIST

TRAVEL QUESTIONS

- Do you bring presents home to family or friends after a vacation?
- Do you get motion sick?
- Do you have a favorite billboard?
- Do you know what to do if there is a flat tire?
- Do you like a sun roof open?
- Do you like to eat in the car?
- Do you like to wear sun glasses in the car?
- Do you like toppings on your ice cream?
- Do you use public bathrooms?
- Did you bring a cell phone and does it have power?
- Do you have a form of identification with you?
- Have you ever been pulled over by a cop?
- Have you ever given money to a stranger on a road trip?
- Have you ever taken a road trip with animals?
- Have you ever gone on a vacation alone?
- Have you ever run out of gas?

- If you could move to any place in the world, where would it be?
- If you could travel anywhere in the world, where would you travel?
- If you could travel in any vehicle, which one would it be?
- If you had three things to wish for from a magic genie, what would they be?
- If you have a driver's license, how many times did it take you to pass the test?
- What are you the most afraid of on vacation?
- What do you want to get away from the most when you are on vacation?
- What foods smell bad to you?
- What item do you bring on ever trip with you away from home?
- What makes you sleepy?
- What song would you love to hear on the radio when you're cruising on the highway?
- What travel job would you want the least?
- What will you miss most while you are away from home?
- What is something you always wanted to try?

>TOURIST

- What is the best road side attraction that you ever saw?
- What is the farthest distance you ever biked?
- What is the farthest distance you ever walked?
- What is the weirdest thing you needed to buy while on vacation?
- What is your favorite candy?
- What is your favorite color car?
- What is your favorite family vacation?
- What is your favorite food?
- What is your favorite gas station drink or food?
- What is your favorite license plate design?
- What is your favorite restaurant?
- What is your favorite smell?
- What is your favorite song?
- What is your favorite sound that nature makes?
- What is your favorite thing to bring home from a vacation?
- What is your favorite vacation with friends?
- What is your favorite way to relax?
- Where is the farthest place you ever traveled in a car?

- Where is the farthest place you ever went North, South, East and West?
- Where is your favorite place in the world?
- Who is your favorite singer?
- Who taught you how to drive?
- Who will you miss the most while you are away?
- Who if the first person you will contact when you get to your destination?
- Who brought you on your first vacation?
- Who likes to travel the most in your life?
- Would you rather be hot or cold?
- Would you rather drive above, below, or at the speed limited?
- Would you rather drive on a highway or a back road?
- Would you rather go on a train or a boat?
- Would you rather go to the beach or the woods?

>TOURIST

TRAVEL BUCKET LIST

1.

2.

3.

4.

5.

6.

7.

8.

9.

10.

>TOURIST

NOTES

Made in United States
Troutdale, OR
03/02/2024